Mindometry

Dancing through the Panic

Damselfly Books 2017

Mindometry

Dancing through the Panic

Wendy Robertson

How do I know what I mean till I see what I say?

I have experienced the blight of so-called Low Mood three times in my life.

The first was when I was fourteen. Nobody noticed this in a busy self-involved household and a busy exam-oriented school. The second time was when for twenty years I'd been a teacher and a lecturer, combining that with writing fiction - as well as a mother, wife and householder after the first two years. This second time it was noticed. I had a very good GP who convinced me that medication could help with what was basically 'a chemical imbalance'.

I helped myself by adjusting my work/life balance, especially by moving onto full time writing and, after eighteen months had passed, I was more of less back to normal and taking no medication.

Twenty years on, during this last winter I've had another spell of this destructive 'Low Mood' thing, plunging into that well remembered darkness when I wasn't looking.(Light is clearly important to my mental welfare.)

This time again I had an excellent GP who recommended medication and some (very good) counselling. The chemicals are doing their work. The good counsellor has helped me draw logical lines through the chaos in my mind. She also showed a real interest in the way that I, as a writer, viewed and was affected by my reactions to this low mood

As I go through my life I have always kept a constant notebook, scribbling ideas, lines, observations, sketches day by day. It has always been so. And these days my notebook is being shaped by my difficult journey through this phase of Low Mood, to the point when I may be able to see a way through.

Then, with the help of the good counsellor I've been enabled to make sense of what might seem to be an incoherent verbal chaos in my mind: to focus on what it all meant. Working on and clarifying the words on the page has meant that I could focus on and clarify the meaning of what I was going through and give it some shape.

This process, with the pills and the benevolent people, is showing me the way back to the steady state of mind that I need to cope with my life.

I have ended up with this collection of developed writing – some from the recent episodes, some from earlier constant notebooks reflecting the same feeling.

Again I say, *How do I know what I mean till I see what I say?*

6

(Inspired by Len Cohen's phrase *'Dance me through the panic' ...)'*

Dance

Strings thrum penetrate your flesh
embracing the unreal
Drumsticks beat around your heart as
you breathe your own distinctive sweat
laced with *Elan* by *Coty.*
Your feet start to stomp, to jump
Your body starts to sway -
your voice sings along, anticipating
a strange new new world, drenched with promise.

Panic

Crowded places, detailed lists,
a thousand colours hit your eye
sidelong looks, curling lips
leaden heart, boiling brain
shaking hands, frozen self
trapped, immobilised, alone
recalling futile actions and
aborted promises -
copping out, settle for less
embracing compromise
haunted by unborn children
surviving behind a wall of glass

Here comes the panic and now there is no dance

BILLY

We walked the path, your giant's hand in mine,
your long fingers poking inside my woollen sleeve .
I remember the nights he left the house, and how
you read the paper as I scaled your knee
settling, birdlike, into that rustling space.
Remember how we cut out pictures
and pasted them in the Panjandrum book
Remember how you read us stories -
your voice going up and down
like a green rocking horse

See now our youngest, somewhat pedantic –
 a family trait -standing tall for Tai Kwan Do, or
white-clad and obliquely oriental -
or cricket-ready, with pads and faceguard

It is a lifetime since
I passed your dying-age of thirty seven
And in that year it dawned on me
how very young you had been to leave your life and mine
with so much life to live. But still, that time
 to my young self you seemed so very old that
it did not feel too terrible. Of course
what was when
I had to learn by heart
just how to seal off the scaring pain

Butter Muslin

I wake up trembling -
time pulsating, tolling
like a church bell

I see you standing there
dressed in yellow, arms raised -
backlit with translucent butter muslin
Visions emerging like stars before my eye -
you at the school gate your hair red, you coat fluffy
You, in sky blue crêpe party dress -
toggled in amber at the neck
You, in your silk dress -
smiling as he stoops, his long his arm
slung like a jacket around your shoulders

You, standing straight and crisp
alone in your blue uniform
silver-buckle-belted

Arrival

The third of four children,

I slipped out barely noticed

among the dogs of war

and other fine distractions.

Later on I made you tea

and passed hard tests,

wrote so many books

just to please your heart

and catch your eye

Shrink

I shrink away from the
careful speech denying need -
the yelling shriek that cries for care;
the empty plate upon the table -
the oven standing there.

But still, I cultivate this
embedded habit of responding
to their reaching hands -
in the end I miss their urgent noise
and can't endure their absence

So I reach out, to touch and
hold them. Truth to tell
I need their clasping hands –
their touch making me
part of the world, theirs and mine.

Siblingometry

Making Prisms of Meaning.

This family is a square:
at each corner is a child -
the hexagon at its centre
surrounds the lynchpin -
the charismatic mother.
The sides of the hexagon
consist of the beloved dead.
and the generations to come,
who send their own stories
whispering onwards and
backwards in time..

Child One: Boy One
She wanted to make you brave like her -
but she should have loved you more.
You are the tender one, your bruised personality
springing out of injury and unintended hurt -
loving music, following fashion
playing out the role of victim
with justified conviction
your hesitancy hiding
a romantic heart
that crashed and broke too early.

Child Two: Girl One
You were the feisty one -
the most like her, with your hot temper
and your challenging demeanour.
She was bound to steal your cigarettes
and smoke them to teach you a lesson
You were bound to be the one to test her to the limits,
to call her grown-up bluff. In the end
you built your wall of worldly success and family life.
So, defeated, she was driven to surrender
her power and ultimately keep her distance.

Child Three Girl Two

You idolised and feared your mother
and tried to please her with cups of tea and
finally with stories inside real books
Needy and watchful, with your eagle-eyes
and bat-like ears, you tried to make sense of the words
and gestures all around you - at first with no understanding.
Even so they stayed with you. Your child-perceptions made
solid
memories which you wove into stories that both hid
and revealed a difficult truth. To know you
the world needs to decode your stories -
fact or fiction – and fabricate its own prisms of meaning

Child Four: Boy Two

You were the last, the final product
of the soul-mated bond cut shattered too early.
You were her baby, her ewe lamb -
So clever and self-determined.
Normally frugal, she'd make any sacrifice for you –(
sweets and bikes galore, showing her pride
and admiration. I remember the day when,
bold as ever, after diving with too much ardour
into the stony shallow river at the bottom of
the bank and came home with
your chest all bloody .

I watched her pick out the small stones
And wind the bandage gently, with a nurse's care.

A Marriage

This marriage went to work
and loved it; it had flowers
in its hair; it wore sober suits
and hippy skirts. It pushed
children in prams and went to parents' meetings.
On seaside holidays it needed two ponchos to
keep warm. It went to the races, to rugby
matches and
to school plays. It waved children off
on their new life and welcomed them back again.
It watched cricket and football. It followed
cop shows on TV. It read newspapers at length.
It read books and wrote them, and posted off
risky manuscripts. It visited clinics and hospitals
and held its breath. This is a marriage that travels
and
continues to relish the boy who eats chocolate
It's a marriage that
still holds hands.

Happiness in Retrospect 1

The Horsebreaker 1

You were happy, then, in the big blue Jag
Driving to Scotland, children singing in the back
their father by your side, aiming for Drummore,
palm-trees in gardens, the sea to the left,
rising land to the right.

You were happy then, at the farm
with its pointed doll's house windows –
its story-book farmer, the man who broke horses -
a brown man, lean, of ancient stock -
and its story-book wife making Royal shortbread

You were happy then, watching the children
playing hide and seek in the garden and going with
the farmer to bring down the cows from the field
to the byre. - watched by their father drinking tea
and reading papers.

You were happy then, in the early evening
watching the farmer break his wild horses -
listening to the high pitched whinny,
the click and clatter of horse hooves in the yard
and the deep voice calling

You were happy then, walking with this lean man
as he marked the bounds of his land
and moving to the very edge of his world.
The white barn owl whooping
Above our heads

The Horsebreaker 11

And here is the man, his clanking boots
Squeezing clover underfoot
A woven whip in his sun-browned hand
His weathered face and hard black eyes
All ready for his morning's work

A horse snickers and canters across -
its coat sporting a rank shine and
steam rising from its broad back.
Its mouth glitters with old sores -
ancient scores, still not settled

No wind, but my face is freshening -
a strange feeling, a burning sensation.
A bird flies up, its wings beating
as, the horsebreaker at my side,
I tramp across the field

.

Later in the day we walk his fields,
march his bounds and
check his walls. He points to the
tumbled stone dwellings and names
his ancient forefathers.

The barn owl swoops -
feral, fluttering –
having spotted his prey
death is the only resolution

Control

Let me be myself,
Let me be myself
Sensual, uncertain
Serious, fumbling, doubting, alone -
sometimes knowing. Funny: too

Be the good girl
Be the good girl
I must stay quiet - never say what I think
Or wonder, or feel, and bite my tongue
 as I watch the stars rise and stain the sky

Always focus on what is before me
resisting the temptation to
surrender to inconvenient
feeling - flare of passion, leading
in quite another direction.

I feel flushed with power
and mental capability
(This strange god in my head)
Then begin to talk with you
of daytime triviality

I smell the sodden leaves
bruising the air with rotten feeling
And merely talk of passing things and
the change in the weather

I have this profound sense of the days
Passing through the millennia
And merely say,
'Oh yes, time does fly,'
'Oh yes! Time does fly.'

La Même

Thinking he was someone else
you leaned down and kissed him
But he wasn't someone else
he was the same -
the same slow delight,
the same pale, bright eyes
the same puckish smile.
But you must admit
he was not the same.
Not the same.

Black Rain

Walking on a wet spring morning
thoughts weighing down
words with a leaden core -
mind too heavy, body more so -
this excess weight
pulling me down

Sky looming, weighed down,
with black rain, waiting.
Now here is the sun, shining down
on sodden grass illuminating my heavy foot-print -
a shining pathway of my mind
unloading dark bitterness
reflected right onto you.

Descartes

You sheltered under a dry stone wall
on the windy side of the moor
sharing the contents of his leather bag:
red wine and round biscuits.
You spoke of thinking and being,
your laughter echoing his,
across drying heathers.
When the storm blew up
you scampered down,
his leather bag over your shoulder,
leaving behind an empty bottle
and the last round biscuit.

Je pense donc je suis.
OR
Cogito ergo sum
OR
I think therefore I am

The Box

Loving me -
don't keep me in a box
tied with golden cords.

Uncertainty is part of
the whole - don't make me
apologise for my insecurity

I accept you as you are -
I want you to
reciprocate

May 21 1966 Age 24

Such Promise

The car was shining new.
You did like your cars. Remember?
You drove me two hundred miles
to the place where you were born -
the street where you played as a child
and the beach where you fished with a long line.
Then we came to the pathway
across from the Grammar School
Didn't you walk there with your father?
Didn't he say, *'The red brick building*
over there will be your gateway to power.
Yes it's complicated. Be sure of that.' ?

Still a Problem

Turmoil in your mind

stops you settling down

to do what you want to do

These are not hard tasks –

simple transcriptions or

straightforward amends. Easy.

But it's like you're made of stone or steel

Lacking the power to move

from sofa to desk.

The Doorway

The sunlight, streaming into the room
Shines onto the grass and the tall trees. Easy to sit here
for three hours and concentrate on a book or a blank,
naked page. Sweeter than the other place.

The other place is a back room with a dark door.
There was a time that she chose this as the perfect workroom
with its living fire, its space for shelves and its tables for papers,
its big computer corner and its sunshine in the afternoon.

But that room became a forbidden place -
darker than this place with
its bright morning sun. She feels that room
holds some strange essence.

She's glimpsed and heard things already in her life
That she knew weren't there. She's no longer reacts to this,
remembering the half-smiles shot in her direction. As a child
she'd been accused more than once of being *away with the gypsies*.

But what about this essence?
Could it be the dread-feeling of some
eighteenth century maid who feared the space?
More likely it's the world flooding in

through the firecracker-gateway of the computer -
a world too vast, packed with too many people,
too many objects, too much pain.
But perhaps this crisis of the door, the room

represents her own guilt for work undone:
tasks un-tackled, obligations unmet,
the long tail of obligation
the compulsion to care.

Or perhaps it's the timid soul
sitting there at her core, not daring
to try to breach that door.
So now, in the window the sunny room

she decides to pull herself together,
get out of the house, away from the door
and away from that essence, that dread-feeling
Wouldn't it be too easy, to stay locked in

and fall asleep yet again?
So she drives out through trees to find
a cool space where she can focus. And begin
to manufacture order out of chaos, to move on again.

New feelings surge through her, begin to dissolve
the visceral strings that tie her down, that
make her dumb and stop her thinking straight.
Now, away from the dull routine and the person

she's become. (She knows she's not that person -
the person she'd invented to meet the low expectations -
in the house with its scary back room
its threatening interior spirit, its emanation of pain).

She's a different person now. She loves the house,
even the room with the dark door. After all these years
they're woven like a crucial thread
in a precious foreign carpet.

The Interlocuter

She: *I see as you say that you're waving your hands towards the floor.*

Me: That's how I feel sometimes. In a place down there. Near the floor.

She: *If you were to call that place something what would you call it?*

Me: I'd call it a dungeon.

She: *How would you describe that dungeon?*

Me: A deep, dark place, its narrow walls are cliffs of coal draped in grey velvet.

She: *Is there light down there? Is there light?*

Me: There's a slit window at the top, framing a bright blue sky. Bright.

She: *How do you feel when you're down there?*

Me: Wooden, frozen. I can't escape.

She: *But you do get out. How do you get out of the dungeon?*

Me: It just happens. I'm there. Then I am out.

(Long pause…)

She: *Could you make a dialogue with the dungeon?*

Me: What?

She: *Could you speak to it. Put your arms around it. Bring it close in to you. Embrace it. You can make it smaller than you. Bring it into your power. It will have to crumble away. Know that place is not, never could be, greater than you.*

Happiness in Retrospect 11

Why I Love France
(Inspired by Leonard's Cohen's eponymous prose piece)

The heat in the morning, the click of rigging and the rustle
of sailing boats setting out for Africa: a long old journey
The wash of the tide against the staithes
Spreading out the seaweed yet again. And again
Francine and Joe wait in the shadows to walk into my story
Pere Goriot walks arm in arm with Jean Valjean
Alongside Jean Sablon and Simone de Beauvoir.
My sandalled feet echo the click of jackboots
And the hollow calls of Jean Moulin

The black church celebrating the sea breathes smoke and
scent
Seagulls, cormorants; a man counting untypical ducks,
their ducklings ticking along behind.
Boys playing swoop into the sea on a tripwire.
Pink sunset catching the tall buildings in relief
Rose red moon rises yet again over…
Moliere, Robespierre, Desmoulins, Baudelaire, Maupassant
inspiring revolutionaries and English poets (Cont'd)

Then there is Paris, all straight lines and elegance. Bateaux
mouches cruise the slumberous Seine,
passing markets like still-lives illustrating a world of plenty.
Men in overalls drink cognac with their morning coffee.
Music and chatter leak out of riverside cafes
and songs gargled with laughter spill across the cobbles
towards the paintings lined up against stone walls of a
church.
In a black dress, pocked with fragrant lavender seeds
a woman tips her ear to the voices of Americans who
have learned to danced in this favourite city.

I love you, France - ,
truly a world of veils and shadows,
pregnant with story.

After-note: *Francine and Joe walked into my novel Writing at the Maison
Bleue. W*

The Ups and Downs of Low Mood

So, you're sailing along, feeling great.

Even greater day by day.

Then you take a dip, a curtsey, a nod to fate,

a dark dip into the black, a mind filled with

storming thoughts: Rachmaninov's brain-fever -

a creeping paranoia that makes the world your enemy

crowded with open mouths, crying and wailing,

demanding attention, Attention.

Achtung! Achtung!

Now for the first time flirting with death.

No. Flirting with an idea of that unspeakable state

brought into being by the recent death of a friend -

I tick off other deaths punctuating my long life,

aqnd go back to the very deepest loss.

There you have it: the great big dip down. Showing that this

is not just a mere chapter setting up the future

but a timely reversal: a dip to keep you grounded

on the way back to normality.

Ends

About Wendy Robertson

Wendy Robertson has written seriously since she was twelve years old, and became a full time writer after twenty years teaching in primary and secondary school and a lecturer in further education. Since then she has had more than twenty novels published as well as two collections of short stories and an occasional articles. Always a storyteller, her wide range of novels reflects her background in history, sociology and psychology. However, as she always says, 'the story is the thing': in her view the force of fiction brings out all kinds of truths.

Having lived in Lancaster and Coventry she now lives with her husband in South Durham in a Victorian house that has featured in more than one of her historical novels. Her son and daughter now work in London and the North, Her daughter carries on the writing tradition with articles for major newspapers and writing books focussing   on lifestyle.

Contact:

email wenrob73@hotmail.com

Blog: http://lifetwicetasted.blogspot.co.uk/

The Bad Child

A new psychological novel from bestselling author Wendy Robertson

We're all experts in childhood. After all weren't we
all once children? But … Twelve year old Dee - is a
misfit in her family. Her parents see her stubborn
wilfulness as a source of chaos in the household.
It's the last straw when she decides not to speak.
As her life begins to unravel Dee tells us her own
story - how she begins to rescue herself from her
own life. But she's not alone on her journey.
Travelling with her is a woman who throws pots
and a dog called Rufus. Then there are Dee's
drawing books and characters she's met in stories
she has read…

Readers' Comments

AJ 'From the first page we have no choice but to
take this fragile but resilient child into our hearts.
We see the world through Dee's eyes, notice
everything as she does, struggling with her 'to work
out what all this means,' from the beasts and cages
that haunt her dreams to the uncomfortable, often
destructive, politics of family life. The world of the
novel is as richly textured as the 'markings,' Dee
makes in her precious books. It is a world in which
the powerlessness of childhood is laid bare. It's
triumph is to show us just how the spirit of the
child survives. What makes this novel so touching
is the way Wendy Robertson fast tracks us straight
into Dee's world'

GJ 'Most striking here is the careful handling of the
mystery of Dee's state of mind and the growing
undercurrent of menace.'

SG 'It's easy to label a child, much harder to see the
real picture. In a tense and moving story, Wendy
Robertson challenges us to find a new way of
looking.'

Made in the USA
Columbia, SC
14 June 2017